December

31-12-18 to 06-01-19

○ 31. MONDAY

PRIORITIES

I0477736

○ 1. TUESDAY

○ 2. WEDNESDAY

TO DO

○ 3. THURSDAY

○ 4. FRIDAY

○ 5. SATURDAY / 6. SUNDAY

January

○ 7. MONDAY

PRIORITIES

○ 8. TUESDAY

○ 9. WEDNESDAY

TO DO

○ 10. THURSDAY

○ 11. FRIDAY

○ 12. SATURDAY / 13. SUNDAY

January

○ 14. MONDAY

PRIORITIES

○ 15. TUESDAY

○ 16. WEDNESDAY

TO DO

○ 17. THURSDAY

○ 18. FRIDAY

○ 19. SATURDAY / 20. SUNDAY

January

Week 4

○ 21. MONDAY

PRIORITIES

_____

_____

○ 22. TUESDAY

_____

_____

_____

_____

○ 23. WEDNESDAY

TO DO

_____

_____

○ 24. THURSDAY

_____

_____

_____

_____

○ 25. FRIDAY

_____

_____

_____

_____

○ 26. SATURDAY / 27. SUNDAY

_____

_____

_____

January

28-01-19 to 03-02-19

○ 28. MONDAY

PRIORITIES

_____

○ 29. TUESDAY

_____

○ 30. WEDNESDAY

TO DO

_____

○ 31. THURSDAY

_____

○ 1. FRIDAY

_____

○ 2. SATURDAY / 3. SUNDAY

February

○ 4. MONDAY

PRIORITIES

○ 5. TUESDAY

○ 6. WEDNESDAY

TO DO

○ 7. THURSDAY

○ 8. FRIDAY

○ 9. SATURDAY / 10. SUNDAY

February

11-02-19 to 17-02-19

○ 11. MONDAY

PRIORITIES

_____

_____

○ 12. TUESDAY

_____

_____

_____

○ 13. WEDNESDAY

TO DO

_____

_____

○ 14. THURSDAY

_____

_____

_____

_____

○ 15. FRIDAY

_____

_____

_____

○ 16. SATURDAY / 17. SUNDAY

_____

_____

_____

February

Week 8

○ 18. MONDAY

PRIORITIES

○ 19. TUESDAY

○ 20. WEDNESDAY

TO DO

○ 21. THURSDAY

○ 22. FRIDAY

○ 23. SATURDAY / 24. SUNDAY

February

○ 25. MONDAY

PRIORITIES

○ 26. TUESDAY

○ 27. WEDNESDAY

TO DO

○ 28. THURSDAY

○ 1. FRIDAY

○ 2. SATURDAY / 3. SUNDAY

March

Week 10

○ 4. MONDAY

PRIORITIES

_____

_____

○ 5. TUESDAY

_____

_____

_____

○ 6. WEDNESDAY

TO DO

_____

_____

○ 7. THURSDAY

_____

_____

_____

_____

○ 8. FRIDAY

_____

_____

_____

○ 9. SATURDAY / 10. SUNDAY

_____

_____

_____

March

○ 11. MONDAY

PRIORITIES

_____

_____

○ 12. TUESDAY

_____

_____

_____

○ 13. WEDNESDAY

TO DO

_____

_____

○ 14. THURSDAY

_____

_____

_____

_____

○ 15. FRIDAY

_____

_____

_____

_____

○ 16. SATURDAY / 17. SUNDAY

_____

_____

_____

March

Week 12

○ 18. MONDAY

PRIORITIES

_____

_____

○ 19. TUESDAY

_____

_____

_____

○ 20. WEDNESDAY

TO DO

_____

_____

○ 21. THURSDAY

_____

_____

_____

_____

○ 22. FRIDAY

_____

_____

_____

○ 23. SATURDAY / 24. SUNDAY

_____

_____

_____

March

Week 13

○ 25. MONDAY

PRIORITIES

_____

_____

○ 26. TUESDAY

_____

_____

_____

_____

○ 27. WEDNESDAY

TO DO

_____

_____

○ 28. THURSDAY

_____

_____

_____

_____

○ 29. FRIDAY

_____

_____

_____

_____

○ 30. SATURDAY / 31. SUNDAY

_____

_____

_____

April

Week 14

○ 1. MONDAY

PRIORITIES

○ 2. TUESDAY

○ 3. WEDNESDAY

TO DO

○ 4. THURSDAY

○ 5. FRIDAY

○ 6. SATURDAY / 7. SUNDAY

April

○ 8. MONDAY

PRIORITIES

○ 9. TUESDAY

○ 10. WEDNESDAY

TO DO

○ 11. THURSDAY

○ 12. FRIDAY

○ 13. SATURDAY / 14. SUNDAY

April

Week 16

15-04-19 to 21-04-19

○ 15. MONDAY

PRIORITIES

○ 16. TUESDAY

○ 17. WEDNESDAY

TO DO

○ 18. THURSDAY

○ 19. FRIDAY

○ 20. SATURDAY / 21. SUNDAY

April

22-04-19 to 28-04-19

○ 22. MONDAY

PRIORITIES

_____

_____

○ 23. TUESDAY

_____

_____

_____

_____

○ 24. WEDNESDAY

TO DO

_____

_____

○ 25. THURSDAY

_____

_____

_____

_____

○ 26. FRIDAY

_____

_____

_____

_____

○ 27. SATURDAY / 28. SUNDAY

_____

_____

_____

April

Week 18

29-04-19 to 05-05-19

○ 29. MONDAY

PRIORITIES

_____

_____

○ 30. TUESDAY

_____

_____

_____

○ 1. WEDNESDAY

TO DO

_____

○ 2. THURSDAY

_____

_____

_____

_____

○ 3. FRIDAY

_____

_____

_____

○ 4. SATURDAY / 5. SUNDAY

_____

_____

_____

May

06–05–19 to 12–05–19

○ 6. MONDAY

PRIORITIES

○ 7. TUESDAY

○ 8. WEDNESDAY

TO DO

○ 9. THURSDAY

○ 10. FRIDAY

○ 11. SATURDAY / 12. SUNDAY

May

Week 20

13-05-19 to 19-05-19

○ 13. MONDAY

PRIORITIES

_____

_____

○ 14. TUESDAY

_____

_____

_____

○ 15. WEDNESDAY

TO DO

_____

○ 16. THURSDAY

_____

_____

_____

_____

○ 17. FRIDAY

_____

_____

_____

○ 18. SATURDAY / 19. SUNDAY

_____

_____

_____

May

20-05-19 to 26-05-19

○ 20. MONDAY

PRIORITIES

_____

○ 21. TUESDAY

_____

○ 22. WEDNESDAY

TO DO

_____

○ 23. THURSDAY

_____

○ 24. FRIDAY

_____

○ 25. SATURDAY / 26. SUNDAY

May

Week 22

○ 27. MONDAY

PRIORITIES

_____

_____

○ 28. TUESDAY

_____

_____

_____

○ 29. WEDNESDAY

TO DO

_____

_____

○ 30. THURSDAY

_____

_____

_____

_____

○ 31. FRIDAY

_____

_____

_____

○ 1. SATURDAY / 2. SUNDAY

_____

_____

_____

June

○ 3. MONDAY

PRIORITIES

○ 4. TUESDAY

○ 5. WEDNESDAY

TO DO

○ 6. THURSDAY

○ 7. FRIDAY

○ 8. SATURDAY / 9. SUNDAY

June

Week 24

10-06-19 to 16-06-19

○ 10. MONDAY

PRIORITIES

○ 11. TUESDAY

○ 12. WEDNESDAY

TO DO

○ 13. THURSDAY

○ 14. FRIDAY

○ 15. SATURDAY / 16. SUNDAY

June

○ 17. MONDAY

PRIORITIES

_____

○ 18. TUESDAY

_____

_____

_____

_____

○ 19. WEDNESDAY

TO DO

_____

○ 20. THURSDAY

_____

_____

_____

_____

○ 21. FRIDAY

_____

_____

_____

_____

○ 22. SATURDAY / 23. SUNDAY

_____

_____

June

Week 26

24-06-19 to 30-06-19

○ 24. MONDAY

PRIORITIES

○ 25. TUESDAY

○ 26. WEDNESDAY

TO DO

○ 27. THURSDAY

○ 28. FRIDAY

○ 29. SATURDAY / 30. SUNDAY

July
Week 27

01-07-19 to 07-07-19

○ 1. MONDAY

PRIORITIES

○ 2. TUESDAY

○ 3. WEDNESDAY

TO DO

○ 4. THURSDAY

○ 5. FRIDAY

○ 6. SATURDAY / 7. SUNDAY

July

Week 28

○ 8. MONDAY

PRIORITIES

_____
_____

○ 9. TUESDAY

_____
_____

_____
_____

○ 10. WEDNESDAY

TO DO

_____
_____

○ 11. THURSDAY

_____
_____

_____
_____

_____

○ 12. FRIDAY

_____
_____

_____
_____

○ 13. SATURDAY / 14. SUNDAY

_____
_____

_____

July

Week 29

○ 15. MONDAY

PRIORITIES
_____
_____
_____
_____
_____

○ 16. TUESDAY

○ 17. WEDNESDAY

TO DO
_____
_____
_____
_____
_____

○ 18. THURSDAY

_____
_____
_____
_____
_____

○ 19. FRIDAY

_____
_____
_____
_____
_____

○ 20. SATURDAY / 21. SUNDAY

_____
_____
_____

July

○ 22. MONDAY

PRIORITIES

_____

_____

○ 23. TUESDAY

_____

_____

_____

○ 24. WEDNESDAY

TO DO

_____

_____

○ 25. THURSDAY

_____

_____

_____

_____

○ 26. FRIDAY

_____

_____

_____

○ 27. SATURDAY / 28. SUNDAY

_____

_____

_____

July

29-07-19 to 04-08-19

○ 29. MONDAY

PRIORITIES

○ 30. TUESDAY

○ 31. WEDNESDAY

TO DO

○ 1. THURSDAY

○ 2. FRIDAY

○ 3. SATURDAY / 4. SUNDAY

August

Week 32

○ 5. MONDAY

PRIORITIES

○ 6. TUESDAY

○ 7. WEDNESDAY

TO DO

○ 8. THURSDAY

○ 9. FRIDAY

○ 10. SATURDAY / 11. SUNDAY

August

Week 33

○ 12. MONDAY

PRIORITIES

○ 13. TUESDAY

○ 14. WEDNESDAY

TO DO

○ 15. THURSDAY

○ 16. FRIDAY

○ 17. SATURDAY / 18. SUNDAY

August

○ 19. MONDAY

PRIORITIES

_____

_____

○ 20. TUESDAY

_____

_____

_____

○ 21. WEDNESDAY

TO DO

_____

_____

○ 22. THURSDAY

_____

_____

_____

○ 23. FRIDAY

_____

_____

_____

○ 24. SATURDAY / 25. SUNDAY

_____

_____

_____

August

26-08-19 to 01-09-19

○ 26. MONDAY

PRIORITIES

_____

_____

○ 27. TUESDAY

_____

_____

_____

_____

○ 28. WEDNESDAY

TO DO

_____

_____

○ 29. THURSDAY

_____

_____

_____

_____

○ 30. FRIDAY

_____

_____

_____

○ 31. SATURDAY / 1. SUNDAY

_____

_____

_____

September

02-09-19 to 08-09-19

○ 2. MONDAY

PRIORITIES

_____

_____

○ 3. TUESDAY

_____

_____

_____

○ 4. WEDNESDAY

TO DO

_____

_____

○ 5. THURSDAY

_____

_____

_____

_____

○ 6. FRIDAY

_____

_____

_____

○ 7. SATURDAY / 8. SUNDAY

_____

_____

_____

September

09-09-19 to 15-09-19

○ 9. MONDAY

PRIORITIES

○ 10. TUESDAY

○ 11. WEDNESDAY

TO DO

○ 12. THURSDAY

○ 13. FRIDAY

○ 14. SATURDAY / 15. SUNDAY

September

Week 38

16-09-19 to 22-09-19

○ 16. MONDAY

PRIORITIES

_____

_____

○ 17. TUESDAY

_____

_____

_____

○ 18. WEDNESDAY

TO DO

_____

○ 19. THURSDAY

_____

_____

_____

○ 20. FRIDAY

_____

_____

_____

○ 21. SATURDAY / 22. SUNDAY

_____

_____

_____

September

23-09-19 to 29-09-19

○ 23. MONDAY

PRIORITIES

○ 24. TUESDAY

○ 25. WEDNESDAY

TO DO

○ 26. THURSDAY

○ 27. FRIDAY

○ 28. SATURDAY / 29. SUNDAY

September

Week 40

30-09-19 to 06-10-19

○ 30. MONDAY

PRIORITIES

○ 1. TUESDAY

○ 2. WEDNESDAY

TO DO

○ 3. THURSDAY

○ 4. FRIDAY

○ 5. SATURDAY / 6. SUNDAY

October

07-10-19 to 13-10-19

○ 7. MONDAY

                                              PRIORITIES

_____

○ 8. TUESDAY

_____

○ 9. WEDNESDAY

                                              TO DO

_____

○ 10. THURSDAY

_____

○ 11. FRIDAY

_____

○ 12. SATURDAY / 13. SUNDAY

October

Week 42

○ 14. MONDAY

PRIORITIES

○ 15. TUESDAY

○ 16. WEDNESDAY

TO DO

○ 17. THURSDAY

○ 18. FRIDAY

○ 19. SATURDAY / 20. SUNDAY

October

Week 43

○ 21. MONDAY

PRIORITIES

_____

_____

○ 22. TUESDAY

_____

_____

_____

○ 23. WEDNESDAY

TO DO

_____

○ 24. THURSDAY

_____

_____

_____

_____

○ 25. FRIDAY

_____

_____

_____

○ 26. SATURDAY / 27. SUNDAY

_____

_____

_____

October

Week 44

28-10-19 to 03-11-19

○ 28. MONDAY

PRIORITIES

_____

_____

○ 29. TUESDAY

_____

_____

_____

○ 30. WEDNESDAY

TO DO

_____

_____

○ 31. THURSDAY

_____

_____

_____

_____

○ 1. FRIDAY

_____

_____

_____

_____

○ 2. SATURDAY / 3. SUNDAY

_____

_____

_____

November

04-11-19 to 10-11-19

○ 4. MONDAY

PRIORITIES

_____

_____

○ 5. TUESDAY

_____

_____

_____

○ 6. WEDNESDAY

TO DO

_____

_____

○ 7. THURSDAY

_____

_____

_____

_____

○ 8. FRIDAY

_____

_____

_____

○ 9. SATURDAY / 10. SUNDAY

_____

_____

_____

November

Week 46

○ 11. MONDAY

PRIORITIES

○ 12. TUESDAY

○ 13. WEDNESDAY

TO DO

○ 14. THURSDAY

○ 15. FRIDAY

○ 16. SATURDAY / 17. SUNDAY

November

18-11-19 to 24-11-19

○ 18. MONDAY

PRIORITIES

_____

_____

○ 19. TUESDAY

_____

_____

_____

_____

○ 20. WEDNESDAY

TO DO

_____

_____

○ 21. THURSDAY

_____

_____

_____

_____

○ 22. FRIDAY

_____

_____

_____

_____

○ 23. SATURDAY / 24. SUNDAY

_____

_____

_____

November

Week 48

○ 25. MONDAY

PRIORITIES

○ 26. TUESDAY

○ 27. WEDNESDAY

TO DO

○ 28. THURSDAY

○ 29. FRIDAY

○ 30. SATURDAY / 1. SUNDAY

December

○ 2. MONDAY

PRIORITIES

○ 3. TUESDAY

○ 4. WEDNESDAY

TO DO

○ 5. THURSDAY

○ 6. FRIDAY

○ 7. SATURDAY / 8. SUNDAY

December

09-12-19 to 15-12-19

○ 9. MONDAY

PRIORITIES

_____

_____

○ 10. TUESDAY

_____

_____

_____

○ 11. WEDNESDAY

TO DO

_____

_____

○ 12. THURSDAY

_____

_____

_____

_____

○ 13. FRIDAY

_____

_____

_____

_____

○ 14. SATURDAY / 15. SUNDAY

_____

_____

_____

December

16-12-19 to 22-12-19

○ 16. MONDAY

PRIORITIES

○ 17. TUESDAY

○ 18. WEDNESDAY

TO DO

○ 19. THURSDAY

○ 20. FRIDAY

○ 21. SATURDAY / 22. SUNDAY

December

Week 52

23-12-19 to 29-12-19

○ 23. MONDAY

PRIORITIES

○ 24. TUESDAY

○ 25. WEDNESDAY

TO DO

○ 26. THURSDAY

○ 27. FRIDAY

○ 28. SATURDAY / 29. SUNDAY

December

30-12-19 to 05-01-20

___

○ 30. MONDAY

PRIORITIES

___

○ 31. TUESDAY

___

○ 1. WEDNESDAY

TO DO

___

○ 2. THURSDAY

___

○ 3. FRIDAY

___

○ 4. SATURDAY / 5. SUNDAY

www.ingramcontent.com/pod-product-compliance
Lightning Source LLC
Chambersburg PA
CBHW071242220526
45468CB00002B/964